driftwood press

literary magazine

Volume Five: Issue Two

Spring 2018

Independently published by Driftwood Press
in the United States of America.

Fonts: Satellite, Garamond, Josefin Sans, & Existence Light.

Cover Image: Richard Vyse
Cover Design: Sally Franckowiak

Digital Edition: April 2018

ISSN 2331-7132

Please visit our website at www.driftwoodpress.net.

Contents

Fiction

Poetry

Visual Art

Fiction

Selected by
James McNulty

Guest Editors:
Rick Krizman

Curse of Ham

Nicholas Nakai Garcia

They had the regalia you'd expect: gold chains, big crosses, and studs in they teeth, jewels dangling, gold rings on ever finger, gold all over like Mansa Musa, little black tears on they cheeks, black tattoos, which I simply don't understand cuz ink dudn't show on black skin. Some kept they sunglasses on—big ones that covered they faces—and, course, they had they britches pulled down, nethergarments wrinkled out for God to see, and they was just as loud as all get out, no mind to other folks set beside them. But they could eat, or so claims Walter. They'un ordered everthin on the menu twice, and he iddn't know where they hid it since every one of them was skin and bones, but, here again, the blacks are that way. It's how they're bred—long and lanky—cuz that's the way Ham must've been when Noah sent him off, and that's a compliment to em. For the rest of how we associate with blacks, well, you heard me tell it already, but here I come to tell it again: the blacks got affinities, and crime aint just a one of em. You've seen the rudeness in mothers who aint a lick of sense till you figure they all screwloose, and kids get so far as fifth grade till they're upsettin the police, and we all heard this kind of story how many times since the mess up in Ferguson. These boys wasn't no different, cuz they were talking about a rap video they aimed to make off in Colfax, Louisiana, and I thought: what in Colfax is there to put on film for? Well, turns out they wanted to film there cuz of the massacre that happened to the blacks in 18-somethin'r other, and they said they goin down there to raise the dead and set em loose on the Earth. For revenge I take it. I asked Walter if he told them boys—since they aint ever cracked a school book—that slavery's been over with a good long while. But Walter said he couldn't get a word in edgewise cuz they was rappers. He said Thelma, who was takin they orders, heard em ramblin curses, and understand this: she like to fell backwards if she iddn't see with her own two eyes one of them boys throwin chicken bones across the table through a ring of salt, mumblin things under his breath like he was overtook. When I heard that I aimed to go down and tell Ms Thelma that they aint done nuthin but truck with the devil on they own souls to get a scare out of her, so she ought not to worry nothin. But

Walter said the second them boys left, he called pastor Lynch down to have a word. I said, Walter, why you'un called Lynch and not sheriff McDermish, and he said it's cuz the law aint a thing to what presence they brung in the diner that night. So Lynch'un went and divined the diner with his hand and a bible, and he come out and said Walter should shut down for a day or two to get the devil out, and Walter was scared enough to do it. He'un closed shop, and I thought, well, this here is serious now, so I went on the internet to look up more about Colfax and what them boys was meant to do out there, and whether I needed to prepare for doom or something like it. I read up on how all them freedmen got killed defending the courthouse, and how the White Legionnaires used a cannon on em all, and how the blacks surrendered, and the whites maimed em, and how they'un dumped all their bodies in the Red River till it dammed. They didn't prod the clog, they just let the mud set atop them till it made a bridge. Readin all that was a mistake. I'un turned the computer off and lay down for bed and had a wicked dream I won't surely forget, cuz there I seen a great big grave dug up, the dirt of it piled like a mountain, the grave so big it was like a stone quarry in the middle of the woods, and there them black boys was standin at the edge of it, rappin into it, enchantin the crypt, and I couldn't see too good as it was nighttime in the dream, but something big rose up from that hole in the world like we do from a bath, and it'un took to walkin across the forest as high as a building stands, and it looked around to get its bearings, and I saw it was a great big black thing, mouth hangin open, its eyes glowin yellow, and it went on walkin into the cities of the south and commenced to steppin all over em, fires eruptin under each step of those barefeet—this colossus negro—and you could see the little traces of the army guns way down below lightin up the dark like morsecode, but they iddnt have no effect cuz he just kept steppin all over us and settin fires, like red hot craters when he lifted his feet, and I knew them rappers was grandbabies of slaves, and they wasn't waitin for no reparations.

On the Moderate Racist:

A Conversation with Nicholas Nakai Garcia

The following conversation was conducted by managing fiction editor James McNulty via email.

James: Hey, Nicholas. Thanks for letting us feature your story. I want to kick off with a few craft-related questions before we move into more socio-political territory. Ready?

Nicholas: Shoot!

James: For first time readers, I should note that Driftwood is not an "accept as is" publication; we work with our fiction writers through multiple drafts to make the story (and by extension, the writer) the best it can possibly be. One of the concessions you, Nicholas, made with me while working on the story had to do with breaking the monologue into multiple sentences. The first draft I saw consisted of a single, long sentence, which I argued was too writerly and not serving the content or the story. Could you talk a little about your initial rationale and why you ended up agreeing that the sentence needed to be broken down?

Nicholas: I always want the prose to reflect the nature of what I'm writing, both in the look of the page and the reader's experience of reading it. For "Curse of Ham," the narrator is prejudiced, superstitious, and addicted to hearsay, so the single sentence was chosen to show a man constantly jumping to conclusions with inability to stop and reflect. I also enjoyed the challenge of trying to make the piece correct, sentence to sentence, without just placing a comma where a period grammatically should be. But after your critique, we decided that the narrator's stampeding rationality would not be lost if we broke up the work here and there. I enjoyed accenting some moments by cutting them off from run-ons, and the run-ons were thus highlighted themselves.

James: Sure. It takes more skill to know where to end a sentence than it does to continue one unendingly, and what you just said about *accentuating* lines by separating them is an important point; often the most revealing lines are the shorter ones that're trying to blend in alongside the longer. Similarly, did you have difficulty with word repetition while trying to keep the momentum in this piece? I'm particularly interested in those moments of transition between thoughts. Any tips for writers regards variation? Getting carried away with conjunctions seems a welcoming pitfall, for instance.

Nicholas: Basically I had "and," "but," and "so" with which to keep the narrator's stampede of consciousness going. I also had access to the southern dialect conjunctions "course," and "here again," but I shaved most of them away after multiple revisions. My only advice about the whole long sentences business is too avoid them because they usually just come across as pretentious, distracting, and unaware that they have been thoroughly conquered by "manly" writers for a long time. I'd hope such gimmicks are only a minor tool in a contemporary writer's box.

James: I'm not whole-heartedly for *avoiding* long sentences as you say—more just that writers shouldn't force them. If you see you're stringing along too many conjunctions, for instance, probably the rhythm is suffering in pursuit of the writerly long sentence; but this isn't to say that all long sentences are writerly and forced. I've often found that the most beautiful sentences I've read and written are rather long. I'm also not sure I see the correlation between masculinity and long sentences. Could you talk a little more about that?

Nicholas: Perhaps if there was no gender bias in literature, women would have an equal amount of long sentences, but writing expedition-style sentences like Franzen, Saramago, Gabriel Garcia Marquez, Faulkner, Beckett, or David Foster Wallace seems to be a literary boy's club endeavor. If not for competition, men sometimes feel they must go on and on to express beauty.

James: You mentioned dialect briefly, too, which is a topic that our own editors are pretty split on. In one camp, there's a belief that any phonetic spelling on the page is pastiche and tacky; whereas the other camp believes it's a noble—if somewhat futile—attempt at realism and accuracy. All of our editors, however, agree that dialect can risk coming off as condescension from the author if not used carefully. Could you give us your viewpoint on dialect in fiction? Why'd you decide to embrace it for this work in particular?

Nicholas: I see both points of view on dialect. I think it requires very careful study in fiction. I wouldn't attempt dialects or accents I haven't grown up with or didn't study in depth. I wrote "Curse of Ham" with a specific dialect because the narrator doesn't say "doesn't." He says "dudn't." If I trust myself to write it like it is, I'm not sure why I would omit it.

James: Where'd you grow up?

Nicholas: I was born and raised in Boulder, Colorado. But my entire family is from Texas.

James: Talk a little about your decision to make this a monologue. Of course, I think it works as a monologue, but I've often heard monologue stories criticized as lazy—avoiding the hard work of fully *showing* and fleshing out what could be better told through a proper, thorough story. Obviously, here at *Driftwood* we think they serve a purpose and shouldn't be abandoned (Rick Hoffman's "The Wandering Woman" [4.1] and Samsun Knight's "The Pharmacist" [4.2] are two other monologues we've published). What do you think you were able to gain from this form that wouldn't have been as successful in a traditionally-shown story?

Nicholas: I think the monologue can easily have an ancient, prophetic, biblical quality, and the style of a story retold sort of "by the campfire" is always more engaging to me.

James: Two of our editors were at first caught off-guard by your use of a dream sequence to wrap up the monologue. Dream sequences are typically regarded as cliché or too on-the-nose, of course. Needless to say, we think this one works for various reasons, which I'll explain; but first I'm more curious to hear your rationale for embracing the dream sequence, as well as if you had any hesitations in doing so.

Nicholas: Approaching a dream even in conversation is sort of rigged because we take dreams for granted. The word "dream" is a deflated representation of a truly psychotic, reality-bending experience. I don't feel comfortable writing about something that can't be seen or heard in the material world. But I wanted to reveal the narrator's horror via revelation, and since I was in first person, the unconscious was the only realm where the things in his vision could be happening.

James: We thought, too, that the dream succeeded in accentuating the theme by complicating it. In the narrator's eyes, the boys are looking for "revenge," not "reparations." I think this is a brilliant move—we expect the Southern narrator to feel bad about the Colfax massacre—and he does—but the primary effect of that guilt is that it makes him more fearful because he thinks those boys deserve revenge and are coming to get it (on him and his). To our editors, this seemed a very sad yet human reaction, and it gave an interesting spin on an unsympathetic character. Could you talk a little about how you came to this development, or, perhaps more broadly, this character?

Nicholas: I come from an All Lives Matter / "I'm not racist, but... " household, yet my mother once slapped my uncle in front of his own children for saying the N-word, and my grandparents championed one of the first integrated youth groups in Memphis during desegregation. The dissonance in my upbringing has led me to think the most common racists are the moderate ones—people who don't want to destroy other races, just accept them on their own terms. In discussions about racism, we're talking largely about these people. So it's more advantageous to represent them in diversity-conscious stories. And I don't think they're hopeless. The agenda in "Curse of Ham" is admittedly exposé, but to enrich it beyond smear, I wanted to show the guilt-fear in supremacy: inheritors evade identifying their freedom from discrimination with the sins of their elders out of fear that it's true and their supremacy will end. Ignorance is aggravating but pitiful. I'd hope that unfolding the "why" of discrimination would allow new approaches for reformation.

James: Sure. The best way to solve a problem is to understand it, after all, and one of the loftiest goals of art is to impart understanding of character—of humans—in a way that psychology textbooks can't. Your last sentence there highlights the value of the unlikable protagonist; the typical bad advice that a protagonist has to be likable is a subscription to the belief in absolute echo chambers—that we need to understand and identify with *everyone* we subject our attention to. Better yet, we should follow around someone like your narrator in an attempt to better understand him, then use that knowledge to prevent his flaws in ourselves or, as you say, attempt new forms of reformation. Does that about cover it?

Nicholas: That about nails it. The bottom line is that people are complex, even the ones we write off, and the better we are at understanding their logic (or illogic), the more effective we can be at getting along.

James: You mentioned earlier that your story has an "agenda." Considering our current president, these "agenda" stories are on the rise. I'd love it if we could delve a little into the benefits and potential dangers of "agenda" stories.

Nicholas: White men, especially in America, might have some new stories left, but I think we should approach our work with a sense of reparations: to represent POC, LGBTQI individuals, and women in traditionally white male roles, represent them as accurately as possible, or expose the inter-workings of white male privilege. I think it's an undeniable duty.

James: Sure. That's one valid, necessary, and noble agenda: better representation of America's diversity in fiction (or more specifically in your example, fiction written by white men). But even within that noble line of thought, nay-sayers would argue that a white male has no business "representing" the LGBTQI community, for instance; or, to get more specific to your story, a "moderate racist" wouldn't appreciate a liberal writer representing him/her. I don't mean to get in the weeds here, but my point is that writing fiction with a clear "agenda" can get into tricky territory because it won't please everyone—some folks may even be offended by well-intentioned gestures. With any tact, of course, a writer will write about *individuals*, not generalized tribes or groups (or perhaps, individuals *within* a tribe or group). But now to bring it all back to "Curse of Ham," do you think you wrote about an individual or a group? Much of what you've said so far suggests the narrator (who doesn't have an *individual* name) represents a group rather than an individual. Do you see any danger in that? Does it risk painting with a broad brush, or is there enough specificity in there to make him an individual *within* a group?

Nicholas: White men still hold a high platform in media, so we need to try and do something right. The more we fail the more we will be corrected. This is good for those of us who are excited to be more inclusive. I wouldn't put a sticker on my work that advertised the content as more ammunition for anyone's bias, but my work is still written with the truths that resonate with me. Everyone has a philosophy whether it's remixed or borrowed. If we care about it, we write about it. For the love of my art, I won't ever try to make my characters vessels for dry pontifications or set them up for other characters to knock down with my own bias. For the narrator in "Curse of Ham," he's a portrait of what one would say in his shoes, seeing what he saw, hearing what he heard. And his words are a conglomeration of things I've heard from people secretly terrified of black culture.

James: So—based on those last two sentences—it seems to me the narrator of "Curse of Ham" is something in-between: both individual (he has a specific experience that is unique to him) and group (he doesn't have an individual name, and his ideas and reactions are clearly meant to represent a group of people) with perhaps weighting in favor of the latter. The specificity of the names (Walter, McDermish, Lynch, Thelma) and the situation seemed to me enough to keep this from being a too-broad, generalized story, but I'm still curious if you can delve a little into the idea of whom is able to represent whom. Earlier, you said you trusted yourself to write from the "moderate" racist's perspective because you'd done your research and grown up around folks like him. But at what point does writing about an individual who belongs to a specific group become writing meant to represent that group? For instance, are liberal writers permitted to represent southern conservatives? Or do they need to be certain that they're not representing the whole group in their writing—rather, they're writing about *one* southern conservative without representing the entire group?

Nicholas: I think these distinctions are up to the reader. It's about familiarity and how much you identify with a character. A lot of people will hear their grandaddies and uncles or fathers in the narrator—or aunts and mothers—just like I do. Does that mean I've stereotyped the southern conservative or nailed a vein of individuals within it? I accept that displaying bigotry in the overused redneck category is easy to write off as dumb parody, but the narrator's poetry of speech and fantastic imagination break the "bumpkin" limitation. This goes back to showing the complexity of disregarded characters that we discussed above.

James: Right—but the "complexity of characters" is what I'd call individualism, as opposed to grouping, and it sounds like we both agree that's what should be strived for in fiction. This also links back to our conversation about dialect. For dialect to work in fiction—for it to avoid seeming like the writer is condescending to his/her characters—the character needs to be shown as relatively bright, or at the very least, complex. Writing dialect surrounding dim or shallow characters results in clear condescension from the writer. Clearly, myself and our editors think you've succeeded in creating a complex, realistic character or we wouldn't have published your work. It isn't enough to write socially aware work; the work has to look at the issue in a complex, thorough way—hopefully by accounting for all sides of the issue. I'm happy to see your work has done that, and after talking with you, it's clear you've put a lot of thought into the story, which I always say is the primary prerequisite for good writing.

Nicholas: Thank you for asking such tough questions. I think having a dialog about these heavy topics is the best way to sculpt great ideas and appropriate philosophies.

James: Absolutely. Conversations—even debates—are crucial to establishing well-informed, well-rounded worldviews. Let's wrap up this interview with a description of the story your work borrows its name from. For readers who aren't aware of the biblical subtext, could you describe the story of Ham?

Nicholas: Sure. Noah had three sons: Shem, Ham, and Japheth, each of whom are claimed to be the prime patriarch of Asia, Africa, and Europe, respectively, in medieval ethnography. One night, Noah punished Ham for seeing him naked by cursing his future bloodlines to serve the descendants of his brothers. Ham is supposedly the father of the Canaanites, an ethnic group the Israelites annihilated citing this curse as vindication. And the slave trade is another atrocity the curse was used to justify. I loved the idea of rotating the curse to be this inevitable revenge where the "Hamitic peoples" (if we're playing by biblical rules) eventually dominate the other two houses. To a man who has benefited from a world built on this curse of subjugation, the sight of successful rappers adorned like kings, who have reclaimed their ancestral rituals without shame, may trigger the panic that the curse is shifting.

James: I think this has been a fruitful conversation, Nicholas. And if any of our readers would like to continue the conversation with either of us, I know we're both eager to do so. Both Nicholas and I can be reached through the contact page on *Driftwood*'s website.

Poetry

Selected by
Jerrod Schwarz
Megan Krupa

Waiting Game

Daniel Kuriakose

Envelopes everywhere.
I asked my dad
where am I to go?
my stomach opens tropical
my face changes in the mirror.
He said follow the birds.
He said when I die
I'll wait for you at the border.

Birds all over.
He said follow the birds.
He said when I die
my face changes in the mirror
Don't die, Dad.
I've wasted too much time for that.
The ring of condensation from the mug.
The feeling of expecting a knock at the door.
Birds all over.
As a kid I tried to get lost in the woods, but never could.

i keep an aquarium

Kiyoko Reidy

the older girls talk about touching themselves
keep your nails short keep your fingers
together keep your knees

where you keep all the pretty things
all the breathing things you know
your body can make

space for orchids and women's work
and a tongue like a trowel too dull
for digging deep enough

to see how you let it get this bad
how you ate nothing
but canned tuna and celery until your teeth

made piles in your palms and
your body got so small it
could be bundled out with the dirty sheets

how no one will kiss you with their mouths
open with their eyes open with
honey on your skin, waiting

for the flies to discover you
for your laugh to become a bulb
burning out for the

koi to do laps of your stomach
scales the color of ripe fruit
it is a dark place for such beautiful fish.

Interview

Kiyoko Reidy

What inspired the poem?

This poem is actually a self-cento. I went back through a bunch of poems of mine that I didn't think were going anywhere, and I picked out some of the lines I liked from each one and tried to fit them together like a puzzle. As soon as I started, I could feel that it was going to work; the pieces were going to come together to make a picture. Because it's a combination of lines from several poems, I feel like this poem takes on a lot of the themes I deal with—sex and pleasure as a woman, mental health, and the way our relationships can cause these things to intersect.

What was the hardest part about writing it? What was the easiest?

The easiest part was picking out all the fun lines! It's really satisfying to go back through old poems and find a way to repurpose them. When you write a lot, you are inevitably going to write poems that you have an emotional attachment to but just don't end up being very good. This allowed me to use some of the moments that worked from those poems. The hardest part was probably finding ways to fit the different lines together in a way that kept the poem interesting but also consistent enough that it felt like all those lines were supposed to go together.

Was there anything in your original conception that did not make it in?

Totally. There were a bunch of lines that just didn't find a place in the poem. A self-cento can't just be the dumping grounds for lines you like but didn't work somewhere else—there's still a lot of crafting that has to go into it. Which, in this case, meant leaving many lines I liked still unused.

Is this poem categorical of your work? Why or why not?

This poem addresses some of the themes that are woven throughout many of my poems, so in that way—yes. It is a good example of the poems that I write. However, I think this poem represents a new direction for me in a lot of ways. In the past, I wrote a lot of "capture this one image/scene" type poems. This poem doesn't do that. Instead, it spends its time searching. That searching is something that has begun to creep into more and more of my poems ever since I wrote "i keep an aquarium" (a positive change, I think). I'm excited to see what new doors this opened and where I'll go from here.

What is your favorite line from the poem or the line you are most proud of?

That's a hard question. I think my favorite line might be "your body got so small / it could be bundled out with the dirty sheets." That image still kind of freaks me out, which I think is a victory.

Is there anything unique about your personal writing process?

That's a hard question! I think everyone writes a little bit differently, but I don't think I do anything especially crazy. I think of most of my poems when I am in motion in some way or another—on runs, during long drives, etc. It's the main time that my brain is able to just roam without purpose, which is so good for creativity.

Who are some of your favorite poets?

Ooh. So many! Right now, I am really enjoying Ada Limón, Ocean Vuong, and Solmaz Sharif.

How long have you been writing poetry? Do you work in any other artistic mediums?

I wrote my first poem when I was six, so I guess I've been writing for about fifteen years. My first poem was about cats, and my second was about mice. I like to think I've made some progress in depth of topics since then, but who can say. I do other types of art, but never as much as I'd like to! I draw, do a little bit of painting, and I play mandolin. I also like crafty stuff—I'm an avid knitter/crocheter.

How would you personally define poetry?

I think poetry is any sort of expression using language. That probably seems like kind of a boring definition, but I want to resist the defining. Whatever I say it is now, someone will come along and do something different and it'll be poetry, too. Poetry is language at its best.

Based on your personal experience, what advice would you give to other writers?

Just keep writing. If you want to pursue a career in the writing world, do it. If you just want to write for yourself, do it. Writing is one of the most cathartic, empowering, and expressive means of self-discovery, but the only way to really get all the benefits that writing can have is to keep doing it. Also, don't take people's opinions on your work too personally. Some people are going to like what you write. Others aren't. That's always going to be the case. You can't please everyone with your writing. Do what feels good to you, don't be afraid to take chances, and just keep writing!

Where can readers find more of your work?

The best place is my blog (poetryandpythagoras.wordpress.com).

What drew you to *Driftwood Press*?

I was going through and reading issues from a bunch of small presses, and *Driftwood* really stood out to me. I was impressed by the caliber of the poems that were being published, as well as the variety in content. I wanted to be in there, too!

To the Park That Was Once a Collapsed Building

Michael Webber

Two nights ago there was a rally within you.
Preachers on soapboxes with megaphones barking
equality, yelps echoed of the relentless
racism. Today, children feed pigeons within you.
No soapboxes uplift, no megaphones speak-out,
only eager bags of bread rest on a bench, ready
to be exhausted or blown away.
Bread thrown to the pigeons while mumbling
bellies shuffle past—squeaking
shopping carts full of other's forgotten
trash, never groceries, and it's far too cold
today to be hungry. Just ask the pigeons. I imagine
shooing the cooing feather dust pans, plucking
bread from their hard-earned beaks, gathering
each crumb among a cigarette-butt minefield.
A dollar store bag my toy sack, doling out
the pain of an overfull stomach,
just ask ole Saint Nick. I imagine feeding
mouths crusted like chalk crime scenes,
open wide to share their graveyard,
cemeteries stingy with headstones—neglected
enamel, all inscribed the same ole epitaph:
Here lies a tongue
A baritone of Happy Birthday & I love thy
A fearless explorer of the shadowed skin upon temples
A famous wrestler of patois & teeth & cheek
A tight rope walker of fleshy pink caves
A pull string doll of "can you spare" or "God bless you"
Died a bloated caretaker of black & yellow piano keys
Death by atrophy too many miles from Carnegie Hall. *(no stanza break)*

Tomorrow a man will sleep on your bench,
but never thank you. Tomorrow a couple will
fight on your checkerboard tables, but never play.
A suit will shoo, *fresh out of change*, jingling on,
whistling how this park was once a building,
how he wished it still was. I disagree,
you were born an esplanade—ivory pews,
tables fluent in monochrome, and vacant steel
trashcans—home to those damned
pigeons who claim your patchy minefield,
now littered with bread.

Interview

Michael Webber

What inspired the poem?

My writing desk used to be on the second floor of my father's dental office, on 78 Court Street in Binghamton, NY. From that vantage, through vast bay windows, I saw all of which came to make this poem. When I first began using this space there was a building nestled up to his. One day this neglected building collapsed onto my father's. After a few months the city thought turning the rubble into a park would be a constructive use of the space. Little did the planners know that a park is more than just an idea—a park needs care and attention. I guess I would say the poem was inspired by neglect and those living on the fringe of society who inhabit our forgotten space.

Where can readers find more of your work?

My poem, "Crab Apples," was published by *Great Lakes Review* (http://-greatlakesreview.org/crab-apples/) and was recently chosen for their annual "best of" print edition.

"I Grew Up Lucky," "The Price of Seasons," and "Lemon Law" were all published by *Triple Cities Carousel* (https://www.carouselrag.com/single-post/2015/12/08/featured-poet-michael-weber).

Who are some of your favorite poets?

Gerald Stern, Stephen Dunn, Gwendolyn Brooks, Jack Gilbert, and Shel Silverstein.

Based on your personal experience, what advice would you give to other writers?

I don't feel as though I'm in a place to give advice necessarily, but I do believe in endurance. That isn't something I feel incompetent to pass along. I persistently assess strengths and weaknesses in my writing—not until this mindset did real progress strike. If a river can be new and the same at every rushing moment, why can't I?

How long have you been writing poetry? Do you work in any other artistic mediums?

I started writing poetry fourteen years ago on guest check pads while working at the Polar Cap ice arena, which ties into the second question—I consider ice hockey my other artistic medium.

What drew you to *Driftwood Press*?

Call me fickle, but I can't help judging a book by its cover.

What is your favorite line from the poem or the line you are most proud of?

"mouths crusted like chalk crime scenes"

How would you personally define poetry?

To me, poetry is anti-meditation meditation—it's less about shutting the world out, and more like opening the doors and turning on every light in the house.

Is there anything unique about your personal writing process?

My writing process took many years of wasted time to become functioning rituals. Computer, coffee, headphones, and a public space—nothing unique there. The divergence is what comes through the ear buds. I find myself getting stuck on a song that relates to my current state, so I generally loop the first ten to twelve wordless seconds and use the repeated melody to drive my work. I could tell you which poems were channeled by which melodies. When editing, I have to play the corresponding looped track to allow myself to revisit that particular mindset. I am currently stuck on "Dark Side of the Gym" by The National.

Offering

Maggie Bailey

For Anders Carlson-Wee

I don't leave the house much.
I'm not even sure I have a body.
Except when I run my hand

over the still angry scar raised
red between my hipbones,
always lower than I expect.

After my son was born they built me
back together with metal staples.
I didn't even notice.

I don't know beauty anymore
or love that burns you to filaments
or sadness that eats its own tail,

thick with salt. No vistas open,
no berries ripen in a dirty hand.
I have my small son's marigold
earwax, my own broken skin.

Today, driving home, both children
crying in the backseat,
I saw a young deer in the median,
pressed into the dip of grass.

She looked asleep
but for the hollowed-out space
below her still furred ribcage.

Interview

Maggie Bailey

What inspired the poem?

Because I am a high school English teacher at a wonderful school, I have the resources to invite poets to visit my classes and give readings. A few years ago, after meeting him at the Sewanee Writers' Conference, I started teaching Anders Carlson-Wee's fantastic chapbook, *Dynamite*, to my seniors. We had read *Into the Wild*, and I wanted to offer them a different vision of freedom and "wildness." Because we somewhat knew each other, I was able to invite Anders to read at my school and he was kind and generous enough to accept. We had a wonderful visit. His work explores a physical submersion in risk and adventure that I, now a mother of two, simply cannot imagine for myself. But I wanted to say, there is still beauty in this other way of living. Knowing Anders from that visit, I knew he would be open to that idea, that offering up of a different beauty. But I think, more importantly, I had to claim it for myself. Other than that, the actual deer really was dead like that in ditch. The poem is a factual cataloguing of my life in way that not all my poems are.

What was the hardest part about writing it? What was the easiest?

The hardest part was giving myself permission to put a C-section in a poem. Once I did, the rest seemed almost waiting to be written.

Is this poem categorical of your work? Why or why not?

Yes, in the sense that I often ground my work in daily observations of nature. Living along the east coast, I do seem to see a lot of deer! That said, this poem more specifically responds to another poet than the rest of my work tends to.

What is your favorite line from the poem or the line you are most proud of?

Weirdly, my favorite line is the image of "my small son's/ marigold earwax." There is so much beauty in the weird details of being a mother, and I am glad I let this one be in a poem. It is hard to grant them that recognition, even though I think they deserve it. A lot of us have been told that babies and bodies don't belong in poems this way. But when you hold a sleeping baby, you get this sweet view of—of all things—their earwax.

Is there anything unique about your personal writing process?

It is terribly unromantic to admit, but I write a lot in Google Docs. That way I can keep track of small thoughts and phrases on my phone, on my laptop at work, or while at home ostensibly doing other work. It keeps my fragments in one place and automatically saves them. Final drafts get hammered out in a word doc or on paper, but those first iterations live in the very unpoetic world of Google Drive.

Who are some of your favorite poets?

Given that I recently got home from AWP in Tampa, this feels almost impossible to answer. Obviously, I think Anders Carlson-Wee is writing urgent and gorgeous work that needs to be read. My first true poetry loves were James Galvin and Louise Glück and I love them still. Otherwise, I am currently enjoying, in no particular order: Mario Chard, Leslie Harrison, Chelsea Rathburn, and Carly Joy Miller. If you aren't following Kaveh Akbar and Emilia Phillips on twitter, you should do so immediately. It's a continual class in how to be a poet and read poetry.

How long have you been writing poetry? Do you work in any other artistic mediums?

I have been writing poetry since I was a little kid, but only after taking classes with Rick Barot when I was in college has my work really sought a level of craft and music that I am still reaching for now. So, almost twenty years by that metric.

How would you personally define poetry?

I think it was Rick Barot, at Stanford, who introduced me to Lorine Niedecker and her image of the "condensery" of the mind. That is how I define what poem is. And he also taught me that the etymological definition of metaphor is *the transfer of burden.* That is what I think a poem does.

Based on your personal experience, what advice would you give to other writers?

The best advice I can offer is to read and appreciate. The more you invest in the writing communities you value, the more meaning this whole endeavor takes on. It can't simply be about accolades—that is not sustainable, on so many levels.

Where can readers find more of your work?

Please visit my website (www.maggieblakebailey.com) and follow me on twitter (@maggiebbpoet).

What drew you to *Driftwood Press*?

Honestly, I liked the name to start (and that map on the homepage). Then I liked the format: poems paired with interviews. Then I read a few issues. One poem I particularly remember liking is "when in rome" by Adam Crittenden. I love it when all those components collide; it really makes me want to be a part of that literary community.

Future Perfect

Heikki Huotari

Love me, love my exoplanet. Love my exoplanet, love my exoplanet's one and only exomoon. Because I can't have what I wanted I'll have special powers that I'll never need to use. Meanwhile my flapping pink flagellum will have moved me through a lime green viscous liquid to my future perfect food.

Interview

Heikki Huotari

What inspired the poem?

I doubt that I know the early history of any of my poems as well as that of "Future Perfect." Tied to a parking meter in front of an apartment building was a bunch of brightly colored balloons, on one of which was printed, "It's a boy." This caused me to reflect on the difference between my current urban and former rural lifestyles. The bright colors caused me to think of the gaudy colors of poison frogs, which I naturally thought to miniaturize and put on a microscope slide and to join, hence to have my own flagella and to use them to move toward my food. The first and second sentences came later during the investigation of the mental state that I thought I might have if I lived in such a simulation.

What was the hardest part about writing it? What was the easiest?

Hardest was discarding the locutions and images that appeared in the poem during the three or four years of its formation, but then stopped singing. Easiest was recognizing and accepting the flow and gestalt of the form of the poem that finally worked.

Is this poem categorical of your work? Why or why not?

I believe it's a good example of my interest in connecting the dots and the maturation, to date, of my practice at so connecting.

What is your favorite line from the poem or the line you are most proud of?

I'm much amused by the second sentence, in that it's such a good example of a poking fun at self-passive-aggressive response to my not getting everything I think I deserve. And I'm pretty sure that amoebae feel that way too.

Is there anything unique about your personal writing process?

Absolutely nothing. Ideas flow past and sometimes I'm fast enough to write one of them down.

Who are some of your favorite poets?

In my previous incarnation (before I became a mathematician) I was influenced by Walt Whitman, James Tate, and Charles Simic. In this life, I'm reading quite a bit of poetry and understanding little, but I have this month been very much enjoying the poems of Julia Story.

Based on your personal experience, what advice would you give to other writers?

Write first, ask questions later, write first, ask questions later, etc. Just keep at it. Also, send your poems out. If they come back, revise, or not, but send them out again.

Where can readers find more of your work?

Google my name, Heikki Huotari, then scroll past the other Heikki or order my first published collection (it costs only $6!) at *After the Pause* (https://afterthepause.com/tag/heikki-huotari/).

What drew you to *Driftwood Press*?

Newpages, Submittable, or Duotrope recommended *Driftwood*, so I had a look. It had (and has) that irresistible new-car smell.

Lucidity in Three Parts (as told by a four year old)

Ahja Fox

I. they take the skeleton first / peel your head like oranges / from sunday school / do you know sunday school? / fingers in boomerangs / and I think his teeth night stalks / the crawl ballerina pretty / so blood red and pinched stars / in the ground / I hear big boys march / stomp birds / stomp ghostless / cupid bows in their cheeks / mommy is laying right here / face covered in a monster's hair / yes / I can be his best friend / but mommy has to die / so he starts a piss flood / pants dancing at his feet / says shhh to my lips / can you say shhh? //

II. I woke up with a river / over me / jackolanterns sad-facing the indian / braids snapped around lamp posts / dirty light picking scabs off the roof / of Africa / beetle bugs / barrette in my barbie's hair / see / she's beautiful / pregnant with all my smiles / my many names / outside / no song / sings the monster / today is steal my shoelaces day / uno cards shredding sky //

III. scrapers of the bathtub / love tasting your smoke / why fire between your lips? / he likes your tattoos / he'll lick them off / candy / slurpee / he is like me / like us / searching the closet for baby flies / we can wear 'em / those twiggy earrings / at the cancer ball / throat in mermaid scales / we can be queens //

Interview

Ahja Fox

What inspired the poem?

This past winter, I visited some family in Texas. My baby cousin (whom I consider my own) came over and stayed with me a few nights while I was there. She knows I am a writer and insisted I write everything she had to say. If I even stopped to take a sip of water, she would start yelling "write my words, write my words." I got five pages worth of her words and it was beautiful. I tucked them away just to keep them but ran into them once I got home. It was two in the morning when some of those words started running through my head. I kept repeating them in different orders and sequences like I was fiddling with puzzle pieces. A poem was written through that fiddling.

What was the hardest part about writing it? What was the easiest?

The hardest part was choosing what to include and what not to include out of five pages of randomness. Also, the order and knowing what form to put the poem in. Every line is a random thought and image that still somehow works all together and I had to keep that in mind when selecting an effective delivery. The easiest part was revising it. I was so focused and determined to make it work when I initially wrote it that I only had to shed some lines, change some word choice, move some things, and check the accuracy and consistency of my form.

Was there anything in your original conception that did not make it in?

When I first started writing it, I kept it light and pretty. Some of the line creations I have now are darker. Honestly, the whole poem is darker, and I made it that way because it showed my energy when listening to my cousin. She is only four, but she was saying some really off the wall stuff that made me feel like she may know and understand things that most parents wouldn't want their kids to. She was so confident in her speech and I wanted that in this poem. Even though I changed a lot of the images and things she said, the vibe of the poem is the same. All of those nice, pink, bubblegum images and lines went in the garbage.

Is this poem categorical of your work? Why or why not?

In content and voice, yes, it is similar to a lot of my other work. I tend to talk about 'dead things,' as in everything has a time it is asleep or dead, and I see beauty in that and like to obsess about it. Bodies, spirits, feelings/emotions, thoughts on something, dreams, what one considers gone or depleted in power or existence. A lot of those dead things are literal in my work. I am also very imagistic which might explain why my brain immediately started trying to make a poem out of a four-year-old's words.

What is your favorite line from the poem or the line you are most proud of?

My favorite is: "I hear big boys march / stomp birds / stomp ghostless / cupid bows in their cheeks /"

I love the way it feels in my mouth. Some of the 'S' sounds hit and some roll.

Is there anything unique about your personal writing process?

I have heard a lot of people say they hate when a writer says their poems come to them in dreams or in some supernatural way to make it sound all magical, but for me it is true. I tell people my poems are ghosts that like to wake me, stalk me, stare me down in the rearview mirror whenever I go out into the world. I am not saying every piece I have ever written started this way; however, a lot of my best or favorites have. Also, I revise in my sleep, and I rework and rehearse lines from my current work in progress in my dreams.

Who are some of your favorite poets?

This is always a hard question. Recent add-ons to my 'I Wish I Wrote It' list are: Heidi Wong (h.w), Charles Bukowski, Danez Smith, Erika Sanchez, and Yusef Komunyakaa.

How long have you been writing poetry? Do you work in any other artistic mediums?

I have been writing poetry since I could write my name. I dabble in painting and multi-media art. I was a dancer for most of my life and hope to get back to that someday.

How would you personally define poetry?

I have always defined poetry as a tub of dismembered limbs (& poetry) or stolen identities.

Based on your personal experience, what advice would you give to other writers?

Go head first. When I was about fourteen, I dropped out of high school because I thought I was going to die. I ended up living and going for my associates at seventeen and graduating. I chose to make my own path and way into my literary community knowing I had less credentials than most people around me. I had to force myself in. It gets hard. I still get discouraged whenever I have to say I am only twenty-one and only have a two-year degree. Some have turned and walked away not understanding how I am where they are. I have gotten here because I just jumped in, I didn't even check the water temperature first.

Where can readers find more of your work?

I always post my publications and performances on my Twitter and/or Instagram (@aefoxx on both sites).

What drew you to *Driftwood Press*?

I heard about it through a friend and started reading. I have read every single issue up to now and I love it. I am honored to be among the other great contributors of *Driftwood Press*.

Violet Hour

Natalya Sukhonos

San Francisco in its violet hour. Fig trees
Breathe with their branches. Phone rings, shrill as a screech owl.
Mama has cancer. Evening, crumpled and tossed. The city shrinks,
Its airy beauty foul. Across the sleeping continent, mama is sick.
Protect the imagination of my soul, Lord —
Her body gone damp as a silver gray rockfish. Blink:
An opal foreknowledge of pain finds its way through my core.
From the shadow of her blind eyes that is like a gem,
Protect me, Lord. From her voice, thinned to a fluty
Whisper. From her abandonment — the soul's home struck
Down, suddenly looted. Beautiful, the black of night, and her old face new.
Dimples dancing in Odessa childhood vineyards.
Mama's face ablaze with theater — students, projects flew
By like specks, the past a beast in hiding from the stars.
Protect me, Lord. Mama has cancer and the wind
Is unforgiving in this city. My phone rings
And I rush to her, to that space where darkness sings.

Interview

Natalya Sukhonos

What inspired the poem?

This poem was inspired by an assignment in my Sound Class at the 92nd Street Y (taught by Rowan Ricardo Williams). The assignment was to take a Shakespeare sonnet, translate it to a foreign language (using GoogleTranslate), then to another foreign language, then to another, and then back to English. We then had to take three lines from this new poem and incorporate them into our poem, adding three colors, three cities, and three animals.

What was the hardest part about writing it? What was the easiest?

The easiest part about the writing process was that it had to follow the whimsical but rigid rules of the assignment. (I translated the Shakespeare sonnet I chose into Russian, Portuguese, and then Bengali). The hardest part about the writing process was that I chose to focus on a really personal, jarring event—finding out via a phone call that my mother has terminal cancer. It was a challenge to transmit the devastation I experienced then without falling into clichés or sentimentality. It was also a challenge playing with time. In the moment when the speaker finds out about the mother's illness, the mother is already undergoing the deep suffering that would mark her final weeks, but she's also in the prime of her youth as a talented theater director in Odessa, Ukraine thirty years prior to her illness. I confess that, like Borges, I don't believe in time.

Was there anything in your original conception that did not make it in?

I had to choose only three lines from the transmogrified sonnet, so most of it didn't make it in, which is probably a good thing.

Is this poem categorical of your work? Why or why not?

The surreal imagery is representative of the way I write. So is the confessional nature of this poem. What's not representative is the borrowing and reworking of Shakespeare's own lines, as well as the adherence to meter.

Is there anything unique about your personal writing process?

I get a glimpse of a line or an image and carry that around with me while I run errands or take care of my daughter. Then, I sit down and write the rest of the poem.

Who are some of your favorite poets?

Mark Strand, Joseph Brodsky, Boris Pasternak, Jack Gilbert, Louise Gluck, Anne Carson, Denise Levertov, Theodore Roethke, Rainer Maria Rilke, Elizabeth Bishop, Anna Akhmatova, Derek Walcott, and e. e. cummings.

How long have you been writing poetry? Do you work in any other artistic mediums?

I've been writing poetry since I was twelve. I used to write in Russian, but now I write in English most of the time. I've been writing more regularly in the last six years, maybe because I'm busier these days. I dabble in visual art (architectural drawings, collage).

How would you personally define poetry?

Loving attention to language. Transforming your wonder at being into a few condensed lines.

Based on your personal experience, what advice would you give to other writers?

Make time for your writing. Meditate. Don't be afraid to write about yourself. Write about cities and trees and children and dreams and fears. Try to get rid of throw-away lines.

Where can readers find more of your work?

"Parachute" was published by *Aldrich Press* (of *Kelsay Books*) and is available on Amazon. I also have some poems on *Really System, The Millions*, and *Saintann's Review.*

What drew you to *Driftwood Press*?

I was interested in the journal because it's a small press with high standards that pays attention to innovative writing.

The President Declared a Public Health Emergency

Erin Carlyle

but the pain clinic is alive and it only wants to bring its children in close. It whispers: *come here, come here little one* then hands my mother her prescriptions. In devotion she sits sleeping—letting out her muscles. She doesn't move—body shrinking. My mother gladly gives up her bones. The clinic suckles my mother's breast then tells her it is her mother. It is her grave-chair—her sweet body-ache. My mother invites me in. She warns me that we will forever throw up and shiver our deaths without the clinic. In its waiting room we pass pills fist to fist while it creatures around us like love.

Laura Palmer Murder Podcast

Erin Carlyle

We watch again the nipple-cut
and blood. The dirt. the deep
creek-secret. Put your knuckle in
the magnolia canopy otherworld.
Turn it to the teeth mark and her
hair messed in plastic wrap
cover. Sit here and take in the dead
women obsession. The girls there all
freckled and water wrinkled.
The low, low woods give memory
to belly-cuts. Listen to the men
there: the dead women. Pull back
the mist to help them climb.
The passage. The bone scatter
of time. She will crawl on her
belly like a worm to entertain you.

Interview

Erin Carlyle

What inspired the poem?

I wrote "Laura Palmer Murder Podcast" after reading an article about Hollywood's obsession with dead women, and that led me to think about my own obsessions with true crime and murder mysteries. When I was around eighteen an acquaintance of mine was murdered, and I've been trying to make sense of that for seventeen years.

For "The President Declared a Public Health Emergency," I was outraged by the current president's indifference to the opioid crisis. My family was completely destroyed by opioids and pharmaceutical drugs. Over the last twenty-five years I have lost connection to my parents and my uncle died as a result of his addiction. This is an issue that has shaped my adult life, and I have just now been brave enough to write about it.

What was the hardest part about writing it? What was the easiest?

Being open about tragic events is always difficult, and trying to craft a "good" poem from something so personal is doubly hard.

Was there anything in your original conception that did not make it in?

I don't think so. I have spent weeks or even months working out the details of a poem, but these two seemed to appear out of nothing.

Is this poem categorical of your work? Why or why not?

I have currently been writing about themes similar to these two poems. Lately I've been nervous to show my writer friends my work because I'm scared they'll think I'm obsessed with dead women, and maybe I am.

Is there anything unique about your personal writing process?

Other than staring at my office wall for hours, I'd say I probably have pretty average writing habits. I also like to switch between writing and looking at pictures of cats.

Who are some of your favorite poets?

Anne Sexton, Margaret Atwood, Cate Marvin, Sarah Rose Nordgren, Natalie Shapero, and Danez Smith. Does Tori Amos count? I'm going to fit her in anyway.

How long have you been writing poetry? Do you work in any other artistic mediums?

I've been writing poetry since I was around eight. I found a book of Emily Dickinson's poetry at the local library and tried to figure it out. I would practice by making my own little poems. I recently rediscovered an old box of my teenage poetry and it's amazingly bad. I've also dabbled in printmaking.

Based on your personal experience, what advice would you give to other writers?

I would tell other writers to make a habit of writing as often as possible and to find other writers to bounce ideas off of. Having a community helps you feel like you're not out there floating in space.

Where can readers find more of your work?

I have a chapbook published by *Dancing Girl Press* titled *You Spit Hills and My Body*.

What drew you to *Driftwood Press*?

I love the work you all publish, and I enjoy the great artwork on the covers. I'm very excited to be published here.

Necromancy

LeeAnn Olivier

The Moon finds the boy's body in a bag stitched
from bulls' bladders

rattling the tree where he hid as a child. It thumps
out, rock-heavy,

a sack of pipes still warm as a pudding skin. She
cradles it to

her brittle ribs, the calf of her limbs, clutching
his awkward bag

of bones, half-lunatic, half-grave. And oh
how strange she

seems with her bulging treasure, her eyes
bits of carnival

glass mimicking the sea, and she coquets,
his resting nook,

his elaborate sarcophagus.

She takes pleasure in his skin puckered
and brown as

figs and covers them both in silk the color
of eggs, all

myth mapped on this sapling, this jewel
on the throat

of the crone Moon silvering her clefts. Bright
puppet, lucent dead.

Interview

LeeAnn Olivier

What inspired the poem?

A good friend of mine disappeared when we were twenty-one, and his body was never found. I had a dream about finding his body wrapped up in a tree. I combined the images from this dream with the myth of Endymion, a young man with whom the moon falls in love. The moon enchants the sleeping Endymion so that he will never wake up, never grow old, and she can always gaze upon him.

What was the hardest part about writing it? What was the easiest?

The hardest part was finding a form that complemented the rhythm, imagery, and subject matter of the lines. The easiest part was probably the first line that came to me immediately after I had the dream.

Was there anything in your original conception that did not make it in?

Yes, I attempted to tell a more complete story of the original myth at first but decided it would be better to stick with imagery rather than trying to make the piece tell a linear, complete narrative.

Is this poem categorical of your work? Why or why not?

Yes. I often write about fairy tales and myths, and image and sound both play an important role in my poetry. The dark tone of the piece is indicative as well.

What is your favorite line from the poem or the line you are most proud of?

I think I like "a sack of pipes still warm as a pudding skin" because of its specificity and its juxtaposition of something that is jarring, even violent, with something that is comforting.

Is there anything unique about your personal writing process?

Sometimes I begin with words rather than with an idea for a larger narrative. On small notecards, I'll write words that evoke a certain mood, subject, or place, and then begin to shuffle them around until lines start to form.

Who are some of your favorite poets?

Lucie Brock-Broido, Donika Kelly, Anne Carson, and Sylvia Plath.

How long have you been writing poetry? Do you work in any other artistic mediums?

I've been writing poetry since I was about five years old—really clumsy attempts at first, I'm sure, but I've always been drawn to the medium. I actually recited a poem about dogs in my school's talent show when I was in the first grade. I also write creative nonfiction and am currently writing a collection of lyric essays with the connecting image of waterways.

How would you personally define poetry?

I think poetry often has more in common with visual art than with other forms of writing. It is a concentration of images and a pure distillation of a larger theme or story. More than other types of writing, poetry evokes a primal or guttural response in the reader, rather than an intellectual or logical one.

Based on your personal experience, what advice would you give to other writers?

Keep a set writing schedule in which you simply show up at the page for a certain amount of time every week regardless of how busy or unmotivated you are. When I actually follow this advice, it allows me to be much more productive.

Where can readers find more of your work?

I have a chapbook called *Spindle, My Spindle* that is available via *Hermeneutic Chaos Press.*

What drew you to *Driftwood Press*?

I like the quality of the work that you publish and its attention to imagery and lyricism.

North Star Marsh

Elizabeth Kerlikowski

A dark cloud of row boat on the pond means food.
Giant catfish churn below. One is blind.
His cataracts and scars: thunder and lightning
on his dark body. We cannot stop
looking down into algal turrets
rainbows wriggling through and brookies.
Gnawed evidence of beaver.
In the row boat we are Earth signs
between elements, soluble and
able to burn like old kapok life vests.
We do not wear life vests.
Seaweed ripples from a snapping turtle's shell.
His mermaid fins stir the water.
Although he is old and missing an eye,
we should avoid falling in.
I used to row far enough from shore
to disappear beneath the lip
of the old wooden skiff before it leaked
to watch the morning scuff light up
or late, sneak out (I kept the oarlocks
oiled up) for fireworks from the camp
at a neighbor lake. Sometimes with the dog.
Mostly alone, shallow as clouds. Beneath me,
I didn't care about, though it supported me.
In this boat's shadow the giant turtle banks,
a slow dance worth waiting for. The pond wears the sky.

Delta 1539

Betsy Johnson-Miller

As the plane uproars through a storm, picture a young man saying, "We open our sanctuaries when there's a disaster." Imagine him feeding the hungry each week. "Afterward, we sing, and because our songs are so beautiful, soon many stay to worship." Picture him next to me, wearing a bracelet carved from a vein of silver, one of the five k's that a Sikh wears upon the body. Imagine him telling me that among the other k's are a turban, a special pair of underwear, and a sword, "because we are warriors." Picture him speaking directly to me now, "Don't worry—we won't die," as we survive another bout of turbulence, and picture me no longer rubbing the silver cross my father gave me before he died. Imagine what was in his paper for his ethics of engineering class. He had to argue whether or not truck drivers should be replaced with artificial intelligence. "It's the number one job in all 50 states. People would lose jobs, but a robot doesn't get tired." Picture a robot, not tired or afraid to fly. Picture a young man who doesn't wait to pray until he gets inside a monstrous bird. Imagine that. We do not tell each other our names.

Visual Arts

Selected by
James McNulty
Jerrod Schwarz

Man Imagines

Richard Vyse

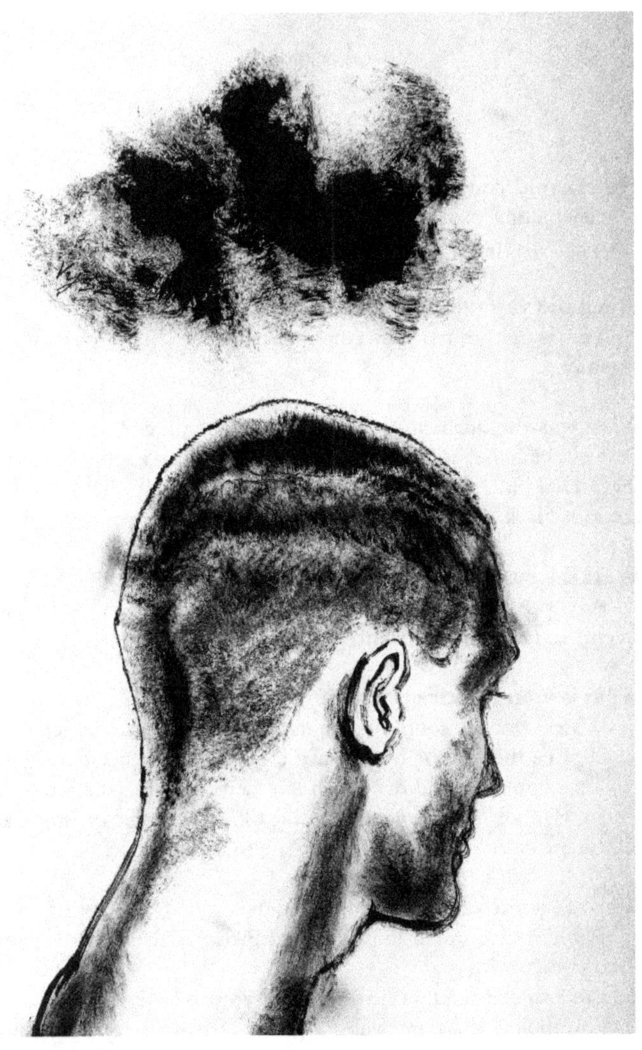

Interview

Richard Vyse

How would you describe your aesthetic?

Celebrating man in art with sensitive line and bold spontaneous brush strokes to capture a moment and a mood.

When did you create "Man Imagines"?

This is one from a series that began in 2017. This art was created in the summer of 2017.

What was the hardest part of crafting this piece?

Searching the internet for a photo to inspire as a reference that had a look that I could interpret and make my own. Deciding whether to create this in color or black and white was also difficult.

Is art the medium you are most invested in?

As a professional commercial artist who has to meet deadlines, it is so freeing to create what I want, when I want.

What is your creative process?

When I find my source of inspiration from the internet, I decide on where I will place the face or figure on the paper. I then decide whether to use a sensitive line or a bold dry brush line depending on the look of the figure. Then, whether to use soft watercolor tones or acrylic brushstrokes depending on the color and mood I am trying to capture.

Who are some of your favorite artists?

Egon Schiele, Auguste Rodin, and Pierre Soulange to name only a few.

Where can our readers find more of your work?

For published art, my website (https://manartbyvyse.blogspot.com).

Photo Submitted as Evidence of a Relationship

Story by
Ray Nayler

Art by
César Sebastian Diaz

CLEAN PAVEMENT,
NOTHING ON THE GROUND,
NO GROUND

BUT CLEAN BLACK ASPHALT
CLEAN WHITE LINES INHABITED

BY CARS STRETCHED
TO HORIZONS.
HE'S LOOKING

PAST THE CAMERA TOWARD
SOMETHING WE CAN'T SEE.

ASPIRATION?
TWILIT CONTRAIL OF AN
EVENING PLANE?
A TREE?
THE SUIT'S NOT HIS:
TOO LARGE
HAIR COMBED AND EVERY
CAR BEHIND HIM LIGHTED UP
IN ROWS OF *CHROME* AND *GLEAM*.

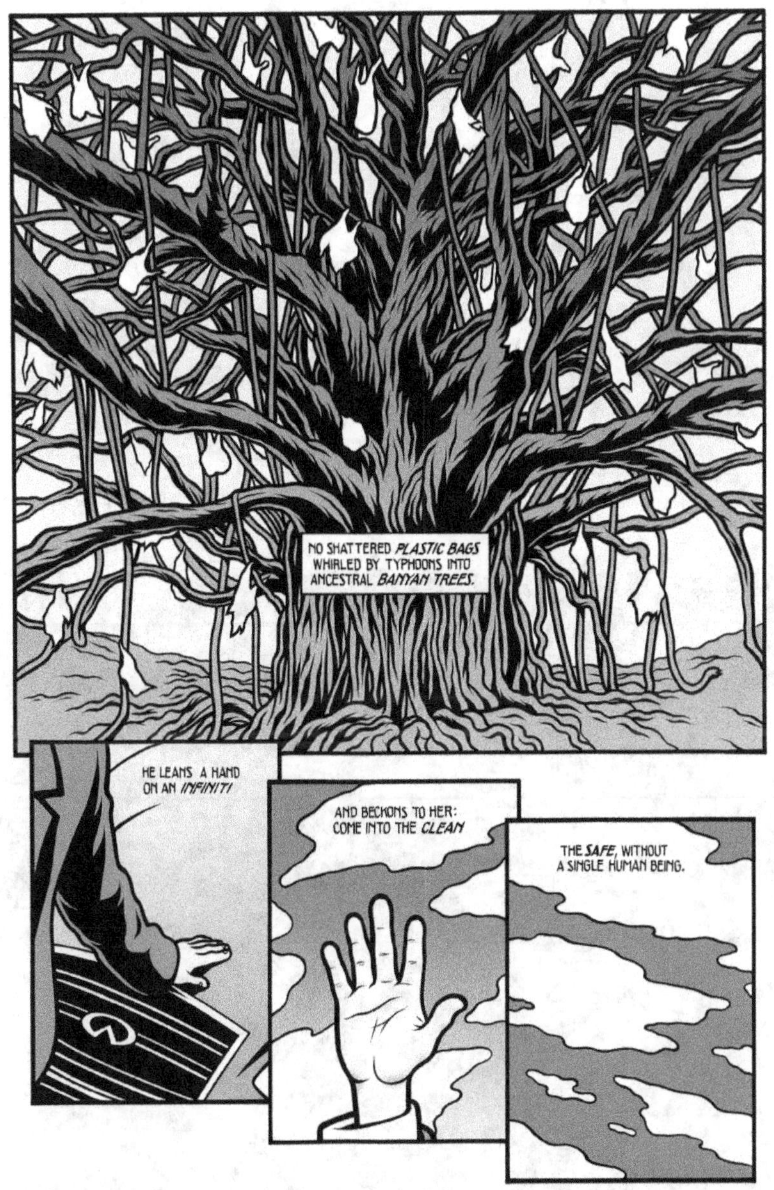
NO SHATTERED PLASTIC BAGS
WHIRLED BY TYPHOONS INTO
ANCESTRAL BANYAN TREES.
HE LEANS A HAND
ON AN INFINITI
AND BECKONS TO HER:
COME INTO THE CLEAN
THE SAFE, WITHOUT
A SINGLE HUMAN BEING.

THE LAND OF VAPOR-LIT, WELL-PARKED MACHINES.
KLIK

www.ingramcontent.com/pod-product-compliance
Lightning Source LLC
Chambersburg PA
CBHW071817190726
48292CB00008B/2880

* 9 7 8 1 9 4 9 0 6 5 0 0 8 *